GW01057531

50 Pearls Of Wisdom
Everything you need to know to be the perfect Mother of the Bride

By Helen Greer

Printed in the United Kingdom

First Printing, 2013

ISBN 978-1483778942

www.50pearls.com

50 Pearls Of Wisdom

Everything you need to know to be the perfect Mother of the Bride

By Helen Greer

Foreword

It's refreshing to find a book that offers useful, straight talking advice for the mother of the bride. 50 Pearls of Wisdom offers advice on everything from choosing the perfect outfit, to tips on how to avoid arguments and stress throughout the planning process. You don't always realise just how much of a toll the whole thing takes on the mother of the bride.

I've stood and listened to thousands of women talking about their experiences as they try on different outfits, but it was a real eye opener for me when I was actually the mother of the bride, finding out just how stressful it can be.

I've seen many trends come and go in my 40 years within the industry. I particularly like how this book encourages you to keep your own style. Choosing an outfit is a matter of individual choice and it should reflect your own personal identity.

What suits one woman, might not necessarily suit you. It's also important to focus on quality. As mother of the bride, a lot of focus will be on you and what you're wearing. You only have one shot at getting it right.

Up until now there's been a distinct lack of advice for the mother of the bride. Not having the resources at your fingertips does make it difficult to know what is expected of you.

50 Pearls of Wisdom will help you to find the perfect outfit and be the best mother of the bride that you can possibly be. By the time you've read it you'll feel more empowered and ready to face whatever your mother of the bride duties throw at you. I really can't recommend this book highly enough.

Joyce Clappison
Wat's On Boutique, Hull
www.wats-on-boutique.co.uk

Introduction

She's actually doing it; your little girl is getting married! While this signals the fact that she's now fully grown up, it's also a time when she's going to need you the most. As mother of the bride you now have a lot of responsibility on your shoulders.

Your daughter is relying upon you to make sure her big day runs as smoothly as possible. Don't panic, by following the simple tips within this book you'll learn how to be the perfect, stress free mother of the bride.

You'll discover:

- How to choose the perfect outfit
- What your main responsibilities will be
- The key to planning a wedding abroad
- How to handle potential problems
- How to deal with your emotions and avoid confrontation
- Financial considerations you need to prepare for

You can't guarantee that problems won't crop up and throw a spanner in the works, but you can be prepared for them. It's a wonderful yet stressful, time consuming and emotionally draining journey you're about to embark on.

These 50 Pearls of Wisdom will help to make the journey a little less bumpy along the way. This is your time to shine. Make sure your daughter has the wedding of her dreams and remember – don't forget the tissues!

𝟙₀ Handling the news

The minute your daughter announces her engagement, you're expected to be happy and supportive. Even if you don't particularly like the groom to be, you need to respect your daughter's decision. She may not appreciate you showing your 'concern' and warning her off. Resist the urge to ask her if she's sure she's making the right decision, give her a big hug and crack open a bottle of bubbly. This is after all, a time to celebrate – your baby is getting married! You can always cry into your tissues later and worry quietly to yourself. Just don't ruin her moment or she might not forgive you for it.

$2.$ Never sacrifice quality for affordability

There are many things you can save on when it comes to the big day. However, your outfit should never be one of them. Quality is much more important than cost; particularly if you plan on wearing it for future occasions. The threads on a low quality outfit will soon start to unravel. Remember, as the mother of the bride you will receive a lot of attention on the big day. You need to ensure you look fantastic, important and distinguishable from other guests. High quality mother of the bride outfits help you to look impeccable, stylish and they will also last for many years to come.

$3.$ Remember: Less is more!

Never has the 'less is more' quote been more fitting. A few accessories are fine, but when you're adding earrings, necklaces, bracelets, hats, heels, handbags and brooches to your outfit, make sure you do not overdo it, you run the risk of looking like mutton dressed as lamb. Now you may look absolutely fabulous for your age, but that doesn't mean you should overdo it with the accessories! Creating a simplistic, yet classy and elegant style is what you want to aim for. After all, you've spent a lot of money on your outfit; why hide it with accessories you don't need?

4. Hat or Fascinator: What's the best option?

The fascinator has dominated the wedding scene over recent years. This modern accessory was made famous in 2011 by the Princess Beatrice of York at the Royal wedding. Speaking of the royal wedding, just take a look at the images of Carole Middleton if you want inspiration. As the mother of the most famous bride in 2011, there was a lot of pressure on Carole to look her best. She managed to pull off a classy, slightly understated look with a beautiful light blue hat. Fascinators can look elegant, but they are mainly a younger fashion. Hats do tend to look better on the mother of the bride, but it's a personal choice. Fascinators can look equally as good and it's better to choose the one that balances with your outfit and you feel most comfortable in.

5. Fittings: Adding up the cost

When trying to come up with a wedding outfit budget, you need to factor in the costs of alterations. Don't worry if you do need an alteration before the big day, but don't even think about skipping this important part to save money. In order to look perfect on the day, you'll need an outfit that is comfortable and that fits perfectly against the body. Even the highest quality, most expensive outfit won't look good if it doesn't fit perfectly. It's common to lose weight (and potentially gain it) before the wedding. Alterations may be needed to accommodate this and the majority of outfits will need one.

6. Aim for elegance, not sexiness

There's nothing more tragic than seeing the mother of the bride trying to be overtly sexy. If you want to embarrass your daughter then by all means, dress provocatively. It's not even about age; you're a mother and on the wedding day you're there as the 'mother of the bride.' This means you need to look like one. Whether you opt for a dress or a two piece outfit, make sure it comes down to the knee and isn't too low cut.

---

7. Order your shoes early – very early!

The very latest you should order your shoes, is three months before the big day. Why is this important? Because you need to wear them in! It's easy to forget just how painful new shoes can be. Unless you wear the shoes in. It will be hard to enjoy yourself when every step sends a shooting pain throughout your entire body. Of course, this doesn't mean you should start wearing them to do your weekly shop! Start wearing them around the house every now and again. That way you won't ruin them or get them dirty and you'll feel comfortable throughout the big day.

𝒮₀ Don't be afraid to copy a look

If you're lacking inspiration for what to wear on the big day, don't be afraid to steal a specific look you've seen. Take a look online and in magazines. All you have to do is a quick image search where you type in "mother of the bride" into google and you'll be presented with hundreds of pictures. Seeing what other people are wearing can help to give you plenty of ideas of what would look good on you. There's no shame in copying a look; just be sure that it's a random person's look, and obviously not someone who will be attending the wedding!

𝒪₀ Avoid prints like the plague

The look you mainly want to opt for is simple and elegant. Busy prints are not a good idea. They tend to go out of fashion pretty quickly and you could end up looking outdated on kept photographs. If you're quite petite this is an especially important rule to follow. Bold, large prints can really take over and drown out your petite figure. If you absolutely insist on prints, opt for subtle stripes, spots or floral prints. If you're opting for bold prints, you'll need to lay off the accessories. Plain, elegant dresses with a sophisticated jacket are one of the best mother of the bride outfits to opt for.

10. Embrace your signature style

More than anything, it's important not to stray too far from your signature style. This is basically the look you are associated with. Every woman has her own unique style; it's what they feel comfortable in. If you aim to change your look dramatically you could end up feeling uncomfortable. Instead, enhance your existing style by choosing a high quality well-fitting outfit. All your daughter cares about is having you there. She doesn't want to see you trying far too hard to impress others. Pick an outfit you feel comfortable and confident in so you can feel great and enjoy the day.

𝟙𝟙. Be prepared for Bridezilla!

It's true what they say – women often become bridezilla when they're planning their own wedding! Even the mildest mannered, most thoughtful, sweet and kind woman can turn into a controllable, emotional, irritable mess when she's planning her special day. Prepare to be shouted at, be a shoulder to cry on and at all times resist the urge to provide your own input unless it's asked for. Let your daughter express how she feels and just remember how stressful wedding planning can be. By the time the happy couple jet off on their honeymoon you'll probably need a holiday yourself!

12. Never under any circumstances, argue over the costs!

You will likely disagree with how much your daughter and her husband-to-be are planning on spending on the big day. However, arguing about the costs of the day and comparing it to your own wedding won't go down well. What you need to remember is that times have changed and the cost of the average UK wedding has now reached more than £18,000. You have to respect her decision. If your daughter wants to spend £2,000 on an ice sculpture in the middle of summer then so be it. Some things just aren't worth arguing about.

13. Accept your emotions

How can she choose pink napkins over beautiful ivory ones? Why can't she see that the invitations would look much better without the italic font? These are just some of the little niggles that can really start to irritate you. If you're starting to argue over the most ridiculous details of the wedding there could be a good reason why. You're watching your baby girl start a new life. It doesn't matter how old she is, to you she's still your baby. Letting her go can be a tough emotional experience. Bottling up those feelings can cause them to emerge in other ways, such as petty arguments. Accept how you feel and what's really behind the cause of your anger. But remember it's her day so go along with what she wants.

14. Don't be afraid of a little shimmer!

There's a common myth that women aged 40+ should avoid shimmering make-up. Granted, if you use too much you could end up looking ridiculous. However, in moderation shimmer can actually be a great tool to make you look fantastic on the day. It helps to give the skin a dewy, fresh look. This will actually make you look younger. Applying primer around the eyes will also help. It smooths out any lines and ensures your make-up doesn't stick. It will also help to keep your make up on all day. The last thing you want to worry about is topping up your make-up.

---

15. Waterproof mascara – an absolute must!

Waterproof mascara is a godsend at weddings. You will cry. There's no getting around it. As soon as you see your little girl in her beautiful dress the tears will start flowing down your cheeks without warning. You need a heavy duty waterproof mascara to stand up to this. If you're having your make-up done professionally on the day then this should already be covered. If you're doing it yourself, waterproof mascaras are easily purchased. If there's just one make-up tip you follow, make sure it's this one!

16. Book yourself in for a spray tan

Often salons do special bridal packages which include the bride, bridesmaids and the mother of the bride. Discounts are given and you can all go together. Going to a tanning salon with your daughter can be a great way to bond before the big day. A nice, light tan can give the skin a healthy glow and make you look up to 10 years younger. The wrong colour however could be disastrous, so make sure you test the salon and the tan they use, on an occasion before the wedding so you can check out its suitability.

---

17. Eliminate those weight worries

There's no greater motivation to lose weight than your daughter's wedding. If you're worried about losing weight before the big day, you have several options. Weight loss groups can provide you with motivation and you will soon start to see results. Whatever you do, avoid fad diets. They may promise to help you lose a lot of weight in a short space of time, but in reality they rarely work. Even if fad diets do work they often leave you with cravings, bad skin and you will also likely end up feeling miserable. This isn't what you want in the lead up to the wedding! Choose a weight loss diet that will suit you.

18. Maintain your own life

As mother of the bride you will likely become involved with a lot of the wedding planning. This can become really stressful. You want to help your daughter, but at the same time it's important to take time out for yourself. Go to a yoga class, meet up with friends and make sure you have your own life. This will help to keep you sane. As soon as you start to feel yourself becoming stressed, take a break. It may help to create a planner of your own, but always remember to take care of yourself.

19. Dress to suit your body type

Sometimes you just have to make the most of what you have. It's unrealistic, not to mention stressful, to think you can completely change your body shape before the big day. Instead focus on finding an outfit that compliments your current body type. No matter what body insecurities you have, there's an outfit out there that can hide your imperfections. High quality designers have a talent for designing and cutting mother of the bride outfits to compliment and flatter women's figures. Dressing for your body shape can really help to ease your weight worries. Specialist mother of the bride stockists are a must if you have any concerns. Remember, day in, day out they dress ladies for special occasions and you can guarantee they've dressed every body shape you can imagine. If you do loose weight and require an alteration, your outfit can be altered a couple of weeks before the wedding for a perfect fit.

20. Keep in contact with the Groom's mother

There are a number of reasons you'll want to get on good terms with the groom's mother. Firstly you'll need to find out what she's wearing. It's important to colour co-ordinate your outfits. It will also help to ease your worries about meeting the in-laws. If you don't know them very well then now's the perfect chance to get to know them. This will make the actual wedding day a lot less stressful. Invite the groom's mother over for dinner, go shopping with her or just keep in contact via the phone. This will help to please your daughter too so it's a win-win situation.

21. Don't feel left out if you are not included in all wedding plans

In the past the mother of the bride planned everything. The daughter just had to worry about turning up. These days however things have drastically changed. You won't always be included in your daughter's wedding plans. This might be a relief, but it can also be a little upsetting. Try not to take it personally. More couples than ever before are taking full charge of their day. Some don't even ask for any input from their parents. This can be for a number of reasons. They could simply prefer it that way, or they could be saving you some of the stress that comes with planning a wedding.

22. Avoid getting defensive

There are so many reasons why mothers and their daughters fall out during the wedding planning process. This could be putting a strain on your relationship. Just because she doesn't completely agree with your suggestions, it doesn't mean she isn't grateful. You won't see eye to eye on everything. It's all about compromise. Learn to listen to your daughter and respect her wishes, rather than taking it as a personal insult. She isn't purposely disagreeing with you; she just may prefer things a certain way.

23. Money talks: Never promise too much!

Traditionally the cost of the wedding was taken care of entirely by the bride's parents. These days' however things have changed. You'll need to work out with your daughter and future son in law, who will be paying for what. Never feel pressured into paying for more than you can afford. Be clear right from the start and say what you are willing to pay for. It could be the flowers, invitations and catering for example. Anything you can contribute towards the big day will be greatly appreciated. You may even find that they don't expect you to pay for anything.

24. Why a loan is a bad idea

It can be tempting to take out a loan to cover the cost of your daughter's wedding. Yes you want to help out, but getting yourself into financial trouble isn't the best way to do that. Some mothers of the bride have even secretly re-mortgaged their house to pay for the fairy-tale wedding. Pay what you can afford towards the day and be honest if you can't afford to fund the entire thing. It's not the 1920's; these days the happy couple often pay for the wedding themselves. Your daughter wouldn't want you to put yourself into financial strain just to pay for her day.

25. Deciding upon a wedding gift

Even if you're paying for the wedding, you'll still be expected to give a gift. If you are paying for the wedding, why not opt for a more sentimental gift? This could be a great idea anyway. Maybe you have a family heirloom you could pass on? Or how about creating a wedding scrapbook? This could contain lots of pictures and stories about the happy couple. If you're quite a crafty person then making something for the newly wedded couple could be a really thoughtful and touching gift. Look online for ideas on unique personalised wedding gifts that they can treasure forever.

$26.$ No strings attached

When paying for parts of the wedding are you expecting anything in return? For example, if you're paying for the band, do you expect them to choose a certain type of band? If you have any conditions that come with paying for the wedding then you need to let your daughter know. Ideally you shouldn't place any conditions on the money. Yes you're paying, but this is your daughter's day. Wouldn't you prefer she had everything she wanted, rather than do things because she feels obligated to you? Make sure all financial intentions are laid out right from the start.

$27.$ Include the groom's parents

While it is traditional for the bride's parents to pay for the day, these days it's not unusual for the grooms parents to chip in too. It's important to make the groom's family feel included too. After all, it's their son's wedding day so they'll be just as excited as you are. They may want to pay for some of the wedding. Unless you talk to them you won't know. Obviously this is a tricky topic to bring up. If you ask them they may feel pressurised into paying. If you do end up paying for everything, be grateful that you were in a position to help.

28. Compliment not compete with The bride!

If you're choosing an outfit yourself, be really careful. You want to compliment the bride's style, not compete against it. Opt for in season colours that will help you to stay stylish and on trend. If you choose a colour that compliments the bride's dress it will also really help to enhance the wedding photos. Take a look at online colour co-ordinator tools for inspiration.

---

29. Let your daughter know you're proud of her

You might not realise it, but your daughter would love your approval for the wedding. It may not be necessarily needed for the wedding to go ahead, but it's definitely something she wants to hear. Set time aside not long after the engagement to spend some quality time with her. Go for a meal together and tell her how proud of her you are. Make sure she knows you have your approval. Even if you don't like the groom to be, tell her you respect her decision and if she's happy that's all that matters. This will strengthen your bond together and make her really happy.

$30.$ Taking care of the invitations

It's traditionally your job to ensure all invitations are sent out. You'll also need to chase up those who haven't yet RSVP'd. It's really important to get replies back from all invitations sent out ASAP. Only once you've got the replies can you start to plan the important stuff like seating arrangements and catering. There should be clear information marked on the invitations as to what date guests will need to confirm by. Don't chase anybody up before that date expires. Some guests will need to try and arrange babysitters so they won't always be able to reply to the invite straight away.

31. Hosting a wedding shower

It used to be extremely bad etiquette for the mother of the bride to host a wedding shower. However, times have changed and these days it is sometimes expected of you. The wedding shower will consist of the bridal party and a few of the bride's close friends. Gifts are given to the bride and the focus is on having fun and celebrating the upcoming wedding. Men don't usually attend this occasion, though again this has changed in recent years. Sometimes it's better to let the chief bridesmaid organise the shower. After all, you already have a lot to do!

32. Church wedding outfits: They don't have to be formal

If your daughter has chosen to have a romantic, traditional church wedding, you may be worried about your outfit – especially if you haven't stepped foot in a church for years! What do you wear to church weddings? The answer is whatever you want (well, within reason). You don't have to turn up in a formal, over the top outfit. As long as you choose a high quality outfit from a top dressmaker, you'll look amazing. Just remember the head attire! This is the most important part of a church wedding outfit. Also remember to cover the shoulders, cleavage and preferably the dress length should be to the knee.

33. Religious style wedding etiquette

If you are not religious, but the bride and/or the groom are, there will be certain religious aspects of the wedding you'll need to find out about. You may be required to light a wedding ceremony candle with the groom's parents. You may also be expected to walk down the aisle afterwards with the father of the bride. This will only present a problem if you are no longer on good speaking terms with your ex. There will be rehearsals so you don't have to worry too much. It's important to respect any religious views the groom and his parents may have.

34. Formal beach and warm climate wedding attire

Beach and warm climate weddings can actually be pretty formal. If you want to find the perfect beach outfit, aim for summer formal occasion wear rather than summer party wear. The only thing you really need to reconsider is a hat. Your head will likely become really hot in the sun. The last thing you want is for you to be too warm and feel uncomfortable. Opt instead for a fascinator or better still, avoid hair accessories altogether!

35. Top tips when shopping for beach and warm climate wedding outfits

Don't be afraid to get your daughter's opinion on your dress. In fact, take her with you while you're looking for the perfect wedding outfit. She'll be able to point out any potential flaws you might have missed with specific outfits. Remember when choosing your shoes that you may be walking on sand. Therefore low heels, or no heels, are the best way to go. Above all else, never leave it until the last minute. Even if you think you'll save money in the sales, you need to purchase your outfit as soon as possible. Do you really want to risk having nothing suitable to wear to your daughter's wedding?

36. Packing for a beach and warm climate wedding

Have you thought about how you are going to transport your outfit? Garment bags are an absolute godsend for transporting dresses and formal outfits. Make sure you keep it with you at all times. This means you'll need to include the outfit in your carry-on luggage. If you place it correctly into a garment bag and fold it once, it should be fit in the overhead bin on the airplane. As well as your main outfit, you should also pack an outfit for the reception. Consider having your make-up applied professionally at the destination. This will limit your hand luggage.

37. Writing your speech

Traditionally the father of the bride gives the speech. However, maybe you need to step in because her father isn't in the picture for whatever reason? Or maybe you'd just like to say a few words of your own as well as your husband? When writing your speech, be sure to welcome the guests and mention your new son in law. Welcome the in-laws to your family too. Don't be afraid to add a little humour here. Above all else, make sure you keep it short and to the point. Finish the speech with a toast to the new married couple.

38. Dealing with the ex-husband (or boyfriend)

If you are no longer with the father of the bride and things didn't exactly end well, now's not the time to re-open old wounds. It can be tempting to start badmouthing your ex to your daughter. Without even meaning to you could find yourself commenting on how you hope he won't be bringing his new girlfriend with him. Even if your daughter doesn't say anything, it is still bound to have an effect on her. This is her day and you are expected to set a good example. You don't have to talk to him, just be civil for your daughter's sake.

39. Hosting the reception

As mother of the bride you'll be the official hostess of the reception. It's your job to welcome each guest to the venue; which means you'll actually need to get to the reception earlier than everyone else. Ideally you want to keep up a good tempo, ensuring everyone gets inside at a good pace. Once the reception's started, your only other duties could include dancing with your new son in law or his father. The chief bridesmaid also tends to have reception duties so you won't be alone. Just focus on enjoying yourself. If you start to get stressed, your daughter will too.

---

40. It's not a competition!

Rivalry between the mother of the bride and the mother of the groom can often break out. Even subconsciously you could be trying to compete with her. It's understandable you want to create a good impression. However, you really need to remember why you are both going to be there. You're both in the same position. Your children are getting married. It's supposed to be a joyous day. Don't ruin it by getting too stressed out on what the mother of the groom is doing or wearing. The only reason you need to know what she's wearing is so you can colour co-ordinate your own outfit.

41. Where to Wear Your Dress Again

The great thing about splashing out on a high quality, well fitted outfit is you can wear it again for other occasions. Race days, fund raisers, corporate events and even dinner dances are all fantastic excuses to get your fabulous mother of the bride outfit out again. This makes it cost effective in the long run. There's also the added benefit that you'll remember your daughter's wedding day each time you wear it. You can tone the outfit down simply by wearing a less formal dinner jacket. You can also add accessories to create a slightly different look too.

42. Don't invite your entire social circle

It's pretty common for the mother of the bride to invite some of her friends to the ceremony and the reception. After all, if you're paying for some, if not all of the wedding, you should at least be able to invite a close friend or two. You need to remember this is your daughter's day. Don't go overboard and invite everyone you know. Yes you want everyone to see your little girl getting married, but will she want them there? Maybe she just wants a small, intimate gathering with only her closest friends and family? Double check with the happy couple first before you start inviting people.

43. Colour coordination is essential

Another very important tip to remember, of which a lot of ladies sadly fail with, is to always match the colour of your hat or fascinator to your outfit. In no circumstances add a different colour hat or fascinator to your outfit, for example a black hat on top of a grey outfit, unless you put the same grey into the hat. Really, your head attire is part of your outfit and not an accessory, so keep the colour the same or a colour that will tone well (e.g a slightly darker or lighter shade of the colour of your outfit). This way, your whole outfit will flow. The idea is for people to look at you as a whole and not see the hat or the outfit first before the other. Just look at the recent family pictures of the christening of HRH Prince George- the Queen and the Duchess of Cambridge look beautifully elegant in their colour coordinating occasion wear attire.

44. Attending the rehearsals

You'll be expected to attend the wedding rehearsals and any pre-wedding parties. Couples usually have between 1-3 rehearsals before the big day. You won't need to wear your wedding outfit for these rehearsals. Just aim to dress smartly; especially if you're going to the church. There will usually be a rehearsal dinner too. The groom's parents will attend this, along with any other close family and friends. It's a great chance to meet the in-laws if you haven't already. You don't have to stress too much about the rehearsals, they're pretty much a relaxed affair.

45. Prepare for potential dinner disasters

You've spent months planning it, but there's always the chance that the dinner could go wrong. Whether you're hosting a formal sit down dinner or a relaxed finger buffet; all kinds of problems can arise on the actual day. The food could be cold, things you ordered could be missing and the service could leave a lot to be desired. Whatever the problem, you need to sort it out ASAP. As soon as you spot a problem, find the catering manager and express your concerns. You'll usually find them to be accommodating and the problems should be fixed fairly quickly.

46. Consider a post-wedding party

If you thrive on playing the hostess, why not host your own post-wedding party? If the reception is due to finish quite early, guests may still feel like carrying on the celebrations. Invite them over to your house or to a suitable venue in order to continue the party. You won't have to worry about food too much. Just provide a few nibbles and plenty of drinks and your guests will be happy. Obviously you'll need to consider the number of guests you can invite back. It may be worth discreetly going around the reception and asking back only select close friends and family.

---

47. Reception order of events

The order of events will differ depending upon what type of reception your daughter is having. A sit down meal reception will usually take around 4 hours. This includes the meal, a cocktail hour, the first dance, champagne toast and speeches, the actual dinner and cake cutting. Once the cake has been cut it's a signal to guests that they can leave whenever they want to. It's the cocktail hour that will be your busiest time as mother of the bride. Guests will come to you with all kinds of questions. Make sure you're wearing comfortable shoes as you'll be on your feet a lot!

48. Providing help to out of town guests

Not all of your guests will live locally. This means they'll need information on accommodation, as well as directions to the venue. You may be expected to book the accommodation for them. The directions and venue information should be sent along with the invitations. This helps people to decide whether or not they can make it before they RSVP. Try to be as helpful as you can be. Don't forget to mention those who have travelled a long way to be there in the speech either. You need to show your gratitude and thank them for sharing in your daughter's special day.

49. Your own religious beliefs may not matter

One of the hardest things you might have to accept is that your religious beliefs may not be welcome at the wedding. Traditionally the mother of the bride could push for the ceremony to be a religious one. These days, unless the bride and groom are religious, there's a high chance you won't be able to change their minds on a religious ceremony. It can be hard to accept this if you've had a fairly strict religious upbringing yourself. You need to work out whether it is worth upsetting your daughter and potentially falling out with her if you push the decision.

50. Put together an emergency kit

An emergency kit for the bride and groom can come in really useful on the big day. Mothers are the queens of being prepared for emergencies. Aspirin, hair pins, tweezers, tissues, corsage pins, dental floss and even a mini sewing kit could come in useful. Even the smallest things that go wrong can send your daughter into a blind panic on her wedding day. So much expectation is placed upon the big day that the slightest problems can spark an emotional meltdown. Be prepared and include everything you think could be needed. It should be small enough to easily fit into your handbag. Chances are if you've got it, you won't need it!

Conclusion

There's no denying that planning for your daughter's wedding can be a tough, stressful experience. However, now you've reached the end of the book you should be a lot more prepared, particularly with what to wear.

Choosing the right outfit can be one of the toughest tasks the mother of the bride faces. Remember, compliment, not compete with the bride and never sacrifice quality for affordability. Your look will receive a lot of attention no matter what colour it is, so choosing the highest quality outfit is essential.

Every mother and daughter relationship is different. While 50 Pearls of Wisdom will help to eliminate worries and prepare you for the big day, it's important you talk to your daughter. Communication is the key to any successful relationship. If something is playing on your mind, talk to her about it. Just remember that this is her day and she just needs her mother there for support.

You've only got one opportunity to get this right. Reading this book has given you the tools you need to be the perfect mother of the bride; you just have to remember them along with everything else. Above all, whatever happens, enjoy the day.

Helen Greer

Printed in Great Britain
by Amazon.co.uk, Ltd.,
Marston Gate.